How To Become A Better Speaker By Changing How You Speak

*Change techniques that will transform
a speech into a memorable event*

*"Practical, proven techniques that will help you to
make your next speech a success"*

Dr. Jim Anderson

Published by:
Blue Elephant Consulting
Tampa, Florida

Printed in the United States of America

Library of Congress Control Number: 2014950749

ISBN-13: 978-1501090349
ISBN-10: 1501090348

Warning – Disclaimer

The purpose of this book is to educate and entertain. This book does not promise or guarantee that anyone following the ideas, tips, suggestions, techniques or strategies will be hired. It is the discretion of employers if you will or will not be hired. The author, publisher and distributor(s) shall have neither liability nor responsibility to anyone with respect to any loss or damage caused, or alleged to be caused, directly or indirectly by the information contained in this book.

Recent Books By The Author

Product Management

- Sales Secrets For Product Managers: Tips & Techniques For Product Managers To Better Understand How To Sell Their Product

- Product Management Secrets: Techniques For Product Managers To Boost Product Sales And Increase Customer Satisfaction

Public Speaking

- How To Give A Great Presentation: Presentation techniques that will transform a speech into a memorable event

- How To Rehearse In Order To Give The Perfect Speech: How to effectively rehearse your next speech to that your message be remembered forever!

CIO Skills

- What CIOs Need To Know About Working With Partners: Techniques For CIOs To Use In Order To Be Able To Successfully Work With Partners

- How CIOs Can Make Innovation Happen: Tips And Techniques For CIOs To Use In Order To Make Innovation Happen In Their IT Department

IT Manager Skills

- How IT Managers Can Make Innovation Happen: Tips And Techniques For IT Managers To Use In Order To Make Innovation Happen In Their Teams

- Secrets Of Effective Leadership For IT Managers: Tips And Techniques That IT Managers Can Use In Order To Develop Leadership Skills

Negotiating

- Learn How To Signal In Your Next Negotiation: How To Develop The Skill Of Effective Signaling In A Negotiation In Order To Get The Best Possible Outcome

- Learn The Skill Of Exploring In A Negotiation: How To Develop The Skill Of Exploring What Is Possible In A Negotiation In Order To Reach The Best Possible Deal

Miscellaneous

- Power Distribution Unit (PDU) Secrets: What Everyone Who Works In A Data Center Needs To Know!

- Making The Jump: How To Land Your Dream Job When You Get Out Of College!

Note: See a complete list of books by Dr. Jim Anderson at the back of this book.

Acknowledgements

Any book like this one is the result of years of real-world work experience. In my over 25 years of working for 7 different firms, I have met countless fantastic people and I've been mentored by some truly exceptional ones. Although I've probably forgotten some of the people who made me the person that I am today, here is my attempt to finally give them the recognition that they so truly deserve:

- Thomas P. Anderson
- Art Puett
- Bobbi Marshall
- Bob Boggs

Dr. Jim Anderson

This book is dedicated to my family: Lori, Maddie, Nick, and Ben. None of this would have been possible without their constant love and support.

Thanks for always believing in me and providing me with the strength to always be willing to go out there and be my best for you.

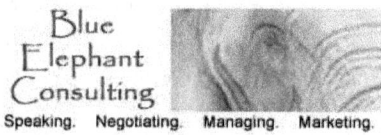

Blue Elephant Consulting
Speaking. Negotiating. Managing. Marketing.

Table Of Contents

How To Become A Better Speaker By Changing How You Speak

As public speakers, the one thing that we all want to be able to learn to do better is to improve how we speak. The challenge that we face is that it's not clear how we can go about doing this. Sometimes we can start to feel trapped and start to believe that we'll never be able to become any better.

The good news is that finding ways to improve our speaking ability is actually fairly simple. The first step in making this happen is to realize that the world is filled with a number of people who do a very good job of speaking public. No matter if we're talking about Jack Welch or Steve Jobs, these people clearly really know how to deliver a speech.

The arrival of modern technology in the form of YouTube has brought speeches by high quality presenters into our homes and offices for the very first time. Now we can sit down, relax and study how the really good speakers make it happen.

Just watching good speakers is not enough. We also have to learn how to slim our speeches down so that they'll fit into the time that we've been allocated. We need to make sure that we don't end up self-sabotaging ourselves. Finally, we also need to take the time to understand what charisma is and how we can work it into our next speech.

This book will show you how to change your speech in order to transform it into something that is even more powerful than it is today. We're going to show you how to find out what you should be doing and how to incorporate the changes that will boost the impact of your speaking.

For more information on what it takes to be a great public speaker, check out my blog, The Accidental Communicator, at:

www.TheAccidentalCommunicator.com

Good luck!

       - Dr. Jim Anderson

About The Author

I must confess that I never set out to be a public speaker. When I went to school, I studied Computer Science and thought that I'd get a nice job programming and that would be that. Well, at least part of that plan worked out!

My first job was working for Boeing on their F/A-18 fighter jet program. I spent my days programming fighter jet software in assembly language and I loved it. The U.S. government decided to save some money and went looking for other countries to sell this plane to. This put me into an unfamiliar role: I started to meet with foreign military officials and I ended up having to give speeches in order to explain what my product did.

Time moved on and so did I. I found myself working for Siemens, the big German telecommunications company. They were making phone switches and selling them to the seven U.S. phone companies. The problem was that the switches were too complicated. Customers couldn't tell the difference between one complicated phone switch from another complicated phone switch. Once again I found myself standing in front of the room giving speeches in order to explain what these complicated machines did and why ours were better than anyone else's.

I've spent over 25 years working as a product manager for both big companies and startups. This has given me an opportunity to do many, many presentations for customers, at conferences, and everywhere in-between.

I now live in Tampa Florida where I spend my time managing my consulting business, Blue Elephant Consulting, teaching college courses at the University of South Florida, and traveling to work with companies like yours to share the knowledge that I have about how to create and deliver powerful and effective speeches.

I'm always available to answer questions and I can be reached at:

Dr. Jim Anderson
Blue Elephant Consulting
Email: jim@BlueElephantConsulting.com
Facebook: http://goo.gl/1TVoK
Web: **www.BlueElephantConsulting.com**

**"Unforgettable communication skills that will
set your ideas free..."**

Create Speeches That Motivate Your Audiences And Get Your Message Heard!

Dr. Jim Anderson is available to provide training and coaching on the topics that are the most important to people who have to speak in public: how can I create a speech that people want to hear and how can I deliver in a way that will allow me to connect with my audience and get my point across to them?

Dr. Anderson believes that in order to both learn and remember what he says, speakers need to laugh. Each one of his speeches is full of fun and humor so that what he says "sticks" with everyone.

Dr. Anderson's Public Speaking Training Includes:

1. How to plan your next speech: pick your purpose and understand your audience.
2. What's the best way to get PowerPoint and Keynote to work with you, not against you?
3. What do you need to do when you are presenting in order to truly connect with your audience?

Dr. Jim Anderson presents over 100 speeches per year. To invite Dr. Anderson to speak at your event, contact him at:

Phone: 813-418-6970 or
Email: jim@BlueElephantConsulting.com

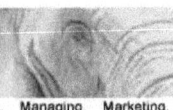

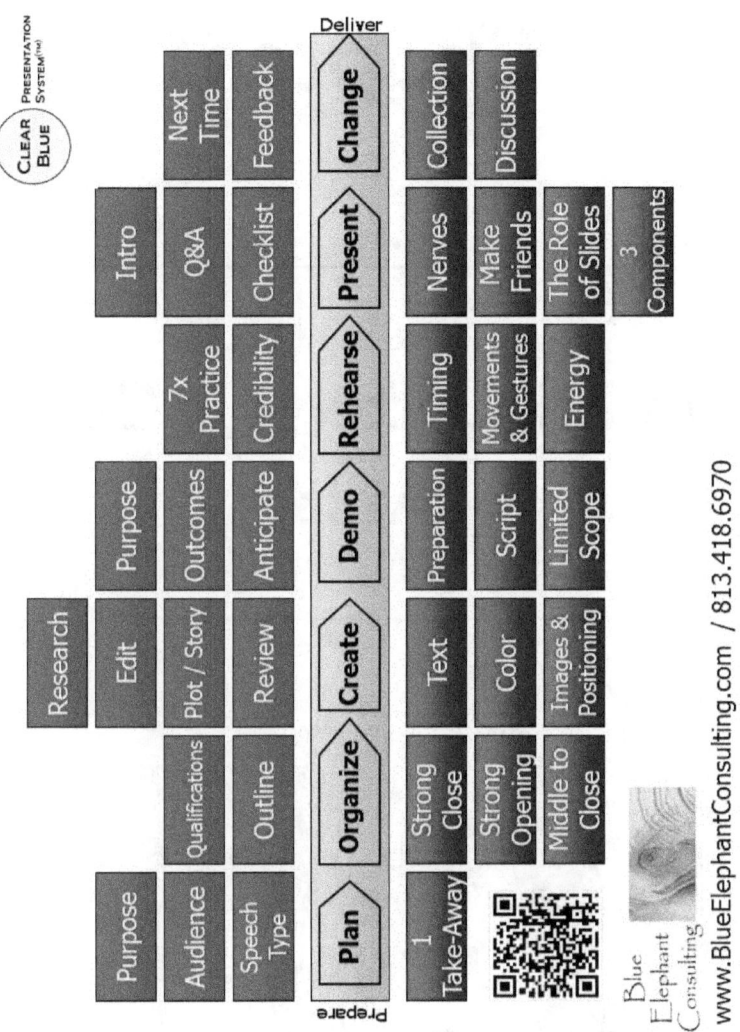

Blue Elephant Consulting has created the **Clear Blue™ Presentation System** for creating and delivering powerful and memorable presentations. The contents of this book are based on lessons learned during the development of the Clear Blue system. Contact Blue Elephant Consulting to learn more about the Clear Blue presentation system.

13

Chapter 1

IM Etiquette: R U Good At It?

Chapter 2

It's Amazing What A Speaker Can Learn By Watching YouTube

Chapter 2: It's Amazing What A Speaker Can Learn By Watching YouTube

Just how does one become a better public speaker? I mean let's be serious here; you do want to get better, don't you? Pretty much any book that you read on the subject or class that you attend in order to build up your skills will tell you the same thing — if you really want to get better, then you've got to take the time to watch the pros at work. Great, just where do you find such pros and how can you get admitted to their speeches to watch them at work? Good news — **I'm going to tell you how (and it's free!)** ...

Welcome To The 21st Century

In the olden days (like about 5 years ago), if you wanted to become a better speaker then yes, you would have to pick yourself up and go to where a good speaker was giving a speech and plop yourself down and start taking notes. Thanks goodness we now live in the modern 21st Century and we no longer have to make such an effort in order **to improve ourselves**.

Carmine Gallo is a communications coach who faced this very problem a few years back. After doing some searching on the Internet, Carmine discovered that the free video service YouTube was a **treasure trove** of recorded examples of excellent speakers. Who knew?

Who Should I Watch?

So now you've found the Library of Congress of online videos. The problem is that there is almost **too much information** here. If you start searching for "speakers", you're going to get blown away. How about if we take a few moments and come up with a list to get you started:

Tony Robbins: people seem to be split on what they think of Tony and his motivational message; however, from a public speaking point-of-view we don't really care — he's one heck of a speaker. His workshops cost thousands of dollars to attend, but on YouTube he's there for you to study for free.

Steve Jobs: Steve was not only a great speaker, but he also had a very good understanding of how to use multimedia to support what he was saying. His presentations at Apple user conferences were legendary for their style and impact. Sure we don't have an army of graphic artists working for us; however, we can learn something from Steve and he was proof that if you practice, practice, practice you will do a good job.

Suze Orman: we all know Suze Orman as a no-nonsense provider of financial advice; however, she's also a fantastic speaker. One of her best qualities is that she handles questions very well — there's no good way to practice for them. Watch and learn!

Looking Beyond YouTube

You might think that once you've found YouTube, that's all that you'll ever need. However, the Internet is a big place and you might be interested in watching **more formal speeches** than you'll be able to find on YouTube. Gallo has done some research and here are some other sites that you should be sure to check out:

Charlierose.com: Charlie Rose is a PBS interviewer who seems to be able to gain access to just about every important person out there. This is the place to go if you want to learn how to master the one-on-one interview.

Cisco: John Chambers, the CEO of Cisco has overcome personal difficulties in order to become a master speaker. His speeches do a fantastic job of making the complicated seem understandable. His trademark move is the trip into the audience in order to connect with people. Watch and learn how a master does it.

Businessweek.com: sure you know about the magazine, but did you know about the web site and its videos? This is where you'll see all of the "big" business leaders being interviewed and you can watch to see how they communicate. Hint: not all of them do a good job of it.

What All Of This Means For You

In the end, we can read all of the books, take all of the courses, and even attend all of the Toastmasters meetings that we can fit into our already busy lives, but in the end it always comes back to one thing: we've got to study and learn from the folks **who know how to deliver a good speech**.

In the old days it required a great deal of effort to seek out who the best speakers were and then to track them down when they were speaking close to where we'd be. However, in today's electronic age, **this is no longer necessary** — now we can bring the speakers to us via the Internet.

In order to make the most of this powerful tool, we need to do our homework. We need to watch each speaker carefully and take good notes on what we think that they do well and where we think that they could do better. These are the notes that we'll then be able to use to **improve our own speeches**. Now go out there and watch some YouTube!

Chapter 3

You Have Much To Learn Grasshopper: What The Great Communicators Can Teach Us

Chapter 3: You Have Much To Learn Grasshopper: What The Great Communicators Can Teach Us

So you've been picked to give a presentation at the next team/department/company gathering. You sit down with a blank computer screen, bring up PowerPoint and as you stare at that blank slide you can almost see your career going into a tailspin and hurtling down towards a flaming crash. Great, now what do you do?

Why would you even think that you know how to give a great presentation? Who taught you how to do this stuff? Jack Welsh? Steve Jobs? John Chambers? Nope, you've probably never talked with them. But you know what, they all do a great job of presenting material. What if they could take you aside for even just a few minutes and have a chat with you. What do you think that they'd tell you to do? Good news – I know and I'm going to share it with you...

Carmine Gallo wrote a book called *Simple Secrets of the World's Greatest Business Communicators*. In this book are the communications tricks that the top business executives use to get their message across. Now you may not yet be the CEO of a major company; however, getting some guidance from folks who are sure couldn't hurt, now could it? Let's take a look at what suggestions we can find in Carmine's book.

- **What would Jack Welch tell you to do?:**
  Jack was the chairman of GE and he did a great job of transforming the company into a world power. Oh, and he cheated on his wife and put some skunky stuff in his retirement package like a fancy apartment paid for by GE, But despite all that, the reason that he was so successful was that he insisted on simple, straightforward communication. Get rid of the jargon

(ROI? CRM? SaaS?) and focus on the basics. Here's a Jack quote for you "Insecure managers create complexity." Jack would tell you to keep it simple, stupid. Got it?

- **What would Steve Jobs tell you to do?**
  Steve was the CEO of Apple and was CEO of Pixar which is now owned by Disney. Dang, what made this guy such a great communicator? At the end of the day, I believe that it was the simple fact that he really, really, really believed in what he was talking about. He was out to change the world and it just seemed to pour out of him. When you watched him talk, you couldn't help but become intoxicated by his message. So here's the question for you: do you believe in what you are going to be talking about? Do you really, really believe in it? Have you figured out how this is going to change the world? You'd better if you really want to captivate your audience. Steve would tell you to make sure that you believe in what you will be talking about.

- **What would Meg Whitman tell you to do?**
  Meg was the CEO of Ebay for ten years. She's worth something like $1.7B – clearly she was quite good at what she did! Ebay was/is all about keeping their customers happy. Meg's gift was that she heavily promoted collecting customer feedback and then taking action on it. Note that she took action – just listening is not enough. Have you listened to the audience that you'll be presenting to? What are they telling you? Have you done this before? What did they tell you that time around? Great business presenters listen before they say a single word. Meg would tell you to get feedback from your audience before you present anything to them.

- **What would John Chambers tell you to do?**
  John is the CEO of Cisco Systems. I seem to recall
  reading somewhere that John has dealt with the
  learning disability of Dyslexia for his entire life. In order
  to prevent it from interfering with his presentations,
  John rehearses over and over and over again for every
  presentation that he's going to give. His rehearsals are
  so detailed that he even practices his walks into the
  audience and placing a hand on someone's shoulder.
  This means that he's able to reel off facts and stats
  about Cisco products without having to even glance at
  his notes. John's presentations are truly a sight to be
  seen. John would tell you to rehearse everything over
  and over again.

Not too bad – now you've had four of the most effective
presenters of our time whisper in your ear what you should do
to deliver a powerful presentation. There's more, but right now
you've got to get to work creating that presentation. Get to it!

Chapter 4

Even More Secrets From The Great Communicators

Chapter 4: Even More Secrets From The Great Communicators

The next time that you are provided with the "opportunity" to deliver a presentation, make sure that you get some advice on how to give a fantastic presentation from today's great business communicators. If you don't have the time (or cash) to fly back and forth between the East and West coasts in order to have sit down discussions with the best of the best, then you have come to the right place.

In this chapter, we're going to touch base with four of today's most powerful communicators and see what suggestions they can offer to you in order to make your next presentation something that everyone will remember (in a positive way) long after you've given it.

We've already chatted with the first four of these "gods of speech". Now let's have a talk with another group of four which includes Michelle Peluso, David Neeleman, Howard Schultz, and Suze Orman.

- **What would Michelle Peluso tell you to do?**
  Michelle is the CEO of Travelocity. Michelle has learned the golden lesson of business management: it's personal. She is famous for having a personal rule that she'll respond to an email from an employee within 24 hours no matter where she is or even if she is on vacation.

  What Michelle understands is that her employees will care about their work if she shows that she cares about them. Michelle's tip for you is to show your audience that you are there for them. How to do this? How about if you sent out an email to everyone who was scheduled to attend your presentation and told them to send you questions before hand so that you could make sure that they got addressed in your presentation. That would be responsiveness!

- **What would David Neeleman tell you to do?**
  David is the Chairman and CEO of Jetblue Airways. Once upon a time David worked for Southwest Airlines (another very good company). In 2002 he founded Jet Blue and make it very similar to Southwest but added perks like in-flight TV.

  David flies Jet Blue to a different city every week. He appears at nearly every first-day orientation for new employees. His real gift is that he is an excellent story teller and he likes to share anecdotes about how Jet Blue employees have risen to the challenge and exceeded expectations. David's tip for you is to remember that we all learn by hearing stories so be sure to tell stories to your audience that inspire them to do what you want them to do.

- **What would Howard Schultz tell you to do?**
  Howard is the chairman of the ubiquitous Starbucks coffee shop chain. Howard really, really, really likes coffee. He is also committed to creating a workplace where all people are treated with dignity and respect.

  Amazingly enough, Howard understands that there is nothing special about Starbucks coffee – rather its competitive advantage comes from the people that it employs. Howard's tip for you is to communicate with passion. Make sure that you identify to your audience and share with them what you are passionate about.

- **What would Suze Orman tell you to do?**
  Suze is an author and a TV show host. She is always

showing up on Public Television fund drives and she has her own TV show on CNBC. Orman has written six consecutive New York Times bestsellers on personal finance.

Suze is upfront in admitting that she's not really passing on any secret information on how to avoid getting crushed by debt, rather it's how she communicates the normally dry and technical information that really counts. Suze's tip for you is to make sure that you express yourself clearly – use simple language to discuss complex issues. Break down complex information into easy parts so that your audience can retain it.

There you go – from their lips (so to speak) to your ears. Your next presentation can only succeed now that you have been given this coaching advice from some of the best communicators out there. But wait, there's more! We all have our own heroes and perhaps I have not yet shared a tip from your personal business communicator hero. If so, the mistake is mine and I'll take care of it in the next chapter...

Chapter 5

Psst: Four More Great Communicators Want To Talk To You

Chapter 5: Psst: Four More Great Communicators Want To Talk To You

If your heart is beating fast, your palms are getting sweaty, and your stomach is not feeling so good, then perhaps you've been asked to give a presentation. Maybe you are normally quite calm and easy going when giving presentations; however, this time around the stakes are just a little bit higher (is the CEO going to be in the audience?). Man, if ever there was a time for a mentor to take you aside and sit you down and tell you what you need to do in order to make this presentation the best ever, this is it! Got any suggestions on how to get out of this bind?

How about if I reach into my bag of world-class great business communicators and ask them to come on over and have a talk with you. We've already had two batches of these folks whisper in your ear. However, we are all motivated by different things and perhaps you have not heard that one tip that you need to make YOUR upcoming presentation the best ever. With your permission, I have a final batch of four great communicators for you to listen to. Sit back, relax, and read away – these folks really know what they are talking about:

- **What would Rudy Giuliani tell you to do?**
  Rudy Giuliani was the mayor of New York City when he became world famous. In the aftermath of the 9/11 attacks he appeared on TV and was able to maintain his composure. His presentation style then and always has been to show true leadership style. The reason that Rudy is so good at what he does is because he is able to make a real emotional connection with his audience.

  One of the primary ways that he does this is by using eye contact to lock in with his audience and make everyone believe that Rudy is just talking to them. Rudy's tip for you would be to spend 90% of your presentation making eye contact with your audience. This is how you'll be able to communicate your emotional message.

- **What would Klaus Kleinfeld tell you to do?**
Klaus was the CEO of Siemens and is now the CEO of Alcoa. His key leadership technique is to create a single vision, set very clear goals to get there, and then communicate the plan to everyone throughout the organization. Whereas there is nothing revolutionary about this, it's HOW he communicates it that makes him unique.

  Klaus gives off an almost insatiable curiosity about everything: his staff, his firm, and the ecosystem in which he does business. Klaus' tip for you would be to take a fresh look at the material that you are presenting. Has your audience heard it all before? If so then reinvent it and present it in a fresh & current way.

- **What would Larry Ellison tell you to do?**
Larry Ellison is the billionaire founder and CEO of Oracle. He spends a lot of time in the bright spotlight of the media whenever he is buying another company, sailing his huge yacht, etc. Larry wins audiences over before he even begins to speak by looking and playing the role of a successful leader.

  Unlike many of his Silicon Valley peers, Larry always looks like a million (billion?) bucks: Italian suits, etc. Larry's tip for you would be to dress just a little bit better than everyone else in the room. If you look like a leader, then you won't have to prove it during your presentation and you can focus on your message. Let your wardrobe do some of the talking for you.

- **What would Richard Branson tell you to do?**
  Richard Branson is another one of those billionaire entrepreneurs who always seems to be in the news. He started with Virgin Music and then moved on to Virgin Airlines and has continued to expand from there. Richard is well known for liking to have fun and the lengths that he'll go to in order to encourage his staff.

  Richard's tip for you would be to be very generous with praise during your presentation. Make sure that employees, customers, and colleagues all get more than their fair share of praise. This will make them feel valuable and make them want to care about your presentation.

Whew! There you go – four more suggestions from the crop of the world's best business communicators. Now go out there and knock 'em dead!

Chapter 6

Presentation Pruning: How Much To Chop?

Chapter 6: Presentation Pruning: How Much To Chop?

Congratulations! You've had been asked to come and present for an hour on a topic that you know a lot about. However, you end up presenting for an hour and a half! Was this a generous gift that you provided of an extra 30 minutes of you talking to your audience or was it a huge social mistake that you took up 30 minutes that weren't yours to take? I believe that the correct answer is (b): if you run over your allotted time, then you've screwed up. What's a presenter to do in order to fit into the available time?

Perhaps a quick discussion about why it's such a great sin to run over your time is in order. Probably the #1 thing to realize here is that your audience will know if you exceed your time. Believe it or not, no matter how wonderful your presentation is they are probably already thinking about what they are going to do AFTER you get done.

If you run over, then all of a sudden you've screwed up their plans and now they resent you for doing that. Going on and on and on really does not impress your audience. Instead, they are going to lose trust in what you are saying. They will start to think that if you didn't take the time to make your presentation the right length, then there is a good possibility that you really don't know what you are talking about in the first place.

So if we can agree that talking too long is a very bad thing, then what is a presenter to do? It's time to do some editing. Now we are all in love with ourselves and how we present information so this can actually be quite difficult to do. One very good way to start the process is to stop for a moment and ask yourself "What am I really trying to accomplish with this speech?"

Remember that the speech is not for you to look good, but rather to cause your audience to be changed in some way. What kind of change are you trying to cause? It's a good thing to keep in mind that the audience is going to be sitting there thinking "What's in this speech for me?" If you can come up with an answer to your question that also answers the audience's question, then you will be in good shape.

Having successfully identified the core reason for giving your speech, now the hard work starts. The best way to determine how long your speech is going to take is to write it out. I personally struggle with this approach a bit because I prefer to outline my speech in order to keep it a little bit more dynamic. However, I do agree that knowing what words you are going to be saying is the best way to determine how long your speech will take.

There are a couple of different ways to shorten a speech. The simplest one is to just start dropping words. However, this won't provide that much of a time savings. Instead, a much better approach is do what Darren La Croix who is a professional speaker does: collapse multiple sentences into a single sentence. This will allow you to reduce the time that your speech takes much quicker.

If after all of this, you find that your speech is STILL too long, then it's time for some more drastic action. Take a look at the number of points that you are making in your speech. Do you have a list of ten things that you are talking about? If so then perhaps it's time to cut that down to a list of 5 things. If it's still too long, then keep on cutting. If you have stories in your speech, then perhaps it's time to drop one or more of them. Stories take time to tell well and this can be a big time saver. The same thing goes for any examples that you are using in your speech – it takes time to lay out and explain an example well and so perhaps it needs to be dropped.

Finally, make sure that you practice. The greatest single factor that can cause a speech to go on too long is if the presenter did not practice his / her speech. This will come through loud and clear to your audience as they see you fumble with words, lose your place, and ramble on. Practice can help you make sure that you are able to present your speech and respect your audience's time.

Chapter 7

_____

SMART Goal Setting Tips For Those Of Us Who Give Presentations

Chapter 7: SMART Goal Setting Tips For Those Of Us Who Give Presentations

So you've given a few presentations (or maybe you've give a lot of 'em). You feel relatively comfortable when you stand in front of a group of people and talk. You may not really like doing this, but you are reasonably sure that you are not going to faint or burst into flames while you are doing it. What's next?

The key to getting better at giving presentation is to dig deep down inside of yourself and find the answer to one very important question: just what are you trying to accomplish?

The answer to this question can be any one of a whole bunch of things. These include acceptance by your peers, more money, a promotion, admiration, or even simply to be seen as being successful by others. There is no wrong answer here – you get to choose what will motivate you to become a better public speaker.

Now it's time to BAG it. Yep, we're talking about crystallizing what drives you and using that to create a Big Audacious Goal (BAG). This is some big presentation goal that you have not yet achieved but that if you became better you could. This BAG goal will serve as a constant reminder as to what you are trying to improve towards with your presentation skills.

If your BAG is where you are trying to get to, then it's time to come up with a way to get there. You may have heard this before but one of the best ways to make measurable progress towards an objective is to set SMART goals for yourself. What does S.M.A.R.T. stand for you ask? Why that must mean that a goal is Specific, Measurable, Attainable, Realistic, and Time-lined. Perhaps a bit of an explanation is required:

- **Specific:** You need to be very clear on exactly what you want to accomplish. "I want to be a better presenter" is too vague. "I want to give 5 more presentations" is very specific.

- **Measurable:** Business loves metrics these days and so do your goals. How are you going to track your progress? If you want to give 5 presentations, then you need to track how many you are giving each month. If a month goes by and you have not presented, then you are falling behind.

- **Attainable:** I call this the Tony Robbins syndrome. If you set a goal to be as good/successful as Tony Robbins, then you are probably going to fail (how many Tony Robbins does the world really need?). However, if you set a goal to be the best presenter in your department, then you just might be able to do this.

- **Realistic:** Once again, let's keep your goals real. If you want to get paid $1M to give speeches to your company, then perhaps you should create a more realistic goal.

- **Time-Lined:** What do you need to accomplish by when in order to make this goal a reality?

There you go – with a BAG and SMART goals you now have the ability to become the presenter that you always dreamed that you could be!

Chapter 8

How To Quickly Move From Good To Great Presentations

Chapter 8: How To Quickly Move From Good To Great Presentations

So why do you care about how good of a presenter you are? Hey, if you've been able to keep from bursting into flames when you address a staff meeting, a department, or even bigger gatherings then haven't you really done enough? For many people, the answer to this question is "yes". And they just leave it at that. But, how about you – are you content to be just "ok". Or would you like to be just a little bit better than everyone else out there?

No matter how well you've done in the rest of your life, how much money you've made, how far you've risen in your career, or how ever else you choose to measure your success by, you can become a great presenter. The only thing that is holding you back is your desire to become better. If you are willing to make the commitment, then you will have made the first step toward presenting greatness.

I hate to say it, but you know what you need to do – you've got to tell someone that you want to become a great presenter. Yeah, yeah, this can be horribly embarrassing – they might think that it's silly and what if you fail?

However, this is a journey that you are starting on and it can become easy to lose your way or to become disheartened after a presentation doesn't go the way that you wanted it to. Having told someone what you are trying to do means that you've made a public commitment and so you are much more likely to stick to it.

So now we move on to the next step: where to look for ways to improve our presenting skills. I'm hoping that I don't have to remind you that Toastmasters is an organization that you really need to join. Keep in mind that there are a lot of really good presenters out there that we can study from.

There are more books, CDs, DVDs, classes, webinars, etc. than you can shake a stick at just waiting for you to show some interest. Additionally, history has shown us who the great presenters were: Woodrow Wilson, Senator Daniel Webster, Winston Churchill, Martin Luther King, etc. Their words and even their speeches have been recorded and are available for you to study. Learn, learn, learn!

I'm almost done, but the one final thought that I'd like to leave you with is to realize that you are sitting on a gold mine of personal stories that can help you move your presentations from good to great. As you improve your technique for delivering presentations, you also need to improve the content of what you are presenting.

This means that you need to make it more interesting. Personal stories always grabs everyone's attention no matter what the topic that you are presenting on is. These are stories that we've not heard before and so we want to know more.

No matter how boring you may think that your life has been, to others it will be a source of endless fascination. Write down the stories that make up your life and then start to study how they can be worked into your presentations. You'll soon go from good to great!

Chapter 9

A Presenter's Greatest Threat: Self-Sabotage!

Chapter 9: A Presenter's Greatest Threat: Self-Sabotage!

A few years back I found myself in a situation where I had allowed myself to get roped into delivering a presentation to a university class. I was going to be talking about what I had learned during my IT career – a somewhat painful and introspective topic. My excitement level was at zero.

I put off creating the speech until the last minute. I threw together some slides the morning of the speech. I ended up showing up just a few minutes before the class started. All three of these actions are not how I do things – what was going on here?

The presentation ended up going ok (everyone clapped at the end). However, I was seriously troubled – why had such a simple speech come so close to being a disaster so many times? After running things through my mind a few times I came to realize that I had been a victim of self-sabotage!

I really, really didn't want to do this speech. It turns out that because of this mind-set, I was working actively to make sure that the speech would never happen (don't write the speech, don't prepare the slides, don't show up). Dang – what was going on here?

Kevin Hogan is both a psychologist and a speaker. His take on all of this is *"Essentially, self-sabotage is consciously or unconsciously blocking yourself from succeeding or accomplishing some task or project."* Well there you go. It turns out that we all have some of this going on, but sometimes it can get out of hand.

What's a presenter to do? First, you need to be aware that you are engaging in self-sabotage. Once you realize that it's happening, you'll be better able to deal with it. Next, use affirmations – tell yourself that you are good at what you are going to be doing. The simple act of saying this to yourself can go a long way. Finally, dig in – focus on what you want to get accomplished and shut out any negative noises that are coming from inside.

It turns out that I must have done better than ok on my presentation to that class because they've asked me back twice a year since then. I now look forward to this presentation because the audience is always appreciative and it gives me a chance to try out new material and techniques. I'm glad that I didn't let self-sabotage do me in!

Chapter 10

Ambush: When Experienced Speakers Develop New Public Speaking Fears

Chapter 10: Ambush: When Experienced Speakers Develop New Public Speaking Fears

Even the most accomplished public speakers can develop a **sudden phobia** about speaking in public. In order to get over this phobia, you need to recognize what kind it is and how to deal with it.

These phobias can show up out of the blue and you'll never see them coming. Judith Pearson is an experienced counselor who has seen this happen time after time and she's got **some suggestions** on what to do if / when this happens to you.

What is a Public Speaking Phobia?

One of the big problems that public speakers have with phobias is simply recognizing them for what they are. It turns out that a sudden fear of public speaking can hit an accomplished speaker at any time. If you find yourself with an **irrational fear** of speaking to a group, then you've got a phobia.

Pearson says that public speaking phobias can be broken down into one of **three main categories**:

- It's all about me
- Past disasters
- Fear of making mistakes in front of an audience

The "It's All About Me" Phobia

In my opinion, this is the most common phobia that can hit an experienced speaker. If you develop this phobia, then all of a sudden you'll find yourself feeling highly **self-conscious** when you think about speaking in public. The more you think about giving a speech, the more you'll feel as though the audience that you'll be talking to will be sitting there disapproving every word that is coming out of your mouth.

The solution to dealing with this phobia is to sit down and have a talk with yourself. You'll need to realize that ultimately it's really **NOT** all about you. In reality, it's the audience that matters – not you. They have come to hear you speak in order to learn – in all honesty it really doesn't matter that you will be the one talking to them.

The "Past Disaster" Phobia

I think that we've all been here before: this phobia is created by some sort of traumatic event that has occurred in your past that had an accompanying highly-charged **negative emotion**. A great example of this would be if something went wrong with a speech and then the event organizer yelled at you about it afterwards.

Once again, the right way to deal with this phobia is to sit down and have a talk with yourself. You need to find a way to make yourself understand that what has happened has happened in the past. You need to realize that it can **never happen again** and you need to move forward. Acknowledge what happened and convince yourself that you'll do better in the future.

The "Fear Of Making Mistakes" Phobia

If you have to have a phobia, then this is probably the one that you'll want to have. The reason is that the fear of making mistakes is really the other side of the desire **to do a great job** at something. The phobia stops you in your tracks or makes it hard to get started because you just don't think that you can do a good enough job at some speaking task.

This is the one phobia that you can actually muscle your way though. Ultimately the solution is to **practice, practice, and practice**. You need to get yourself to a point where you can realize that you are always going to make mistakes (we're all human after all). However, you need to be able to observe your mistakes when you make them, make corrections, and then continue on.

Final Thoughts

Phobias are not just for beginning speakers – they can hit any of us at any time. The key to dealing with a public speaking phobia is to realize what it is – an **irrational fear**.

Dealing with the three most common forms of public speaking phobias requires you to sit down and think through your fears in order to put them in context. This is the best way for dealing with them. Learn to do this well and you'll be able to intimately connect with your audience and make a **lasting impact** in their lives.

Chapter 11

Real World Speaking: A Trip To See The Doctor

Chapter 11: Real World Speaking: A Trip To See The Doctor

We can talk about how to give great speeches until we are blue in the face; however, it ultimately comes down to just how well all of the things that we've discussed are **put into practice** that will determine how effective our talks are.

I recently had a chance to attend a series of presentations that were talking about the U.S. healthcare system. This gave me a unique opportunity to watch some very well educated folks do their best to give a good speech. Come along with me and we'll see how they did...

Pam Arlotto

Pam Arlotto Speaks

Pam has **great credentials**: she is a big player in the healthcare field having been a past president of the HIMSS organization and currently being an advisor to the CCHIT. What missed right off the bat was that her introduction didn't do her credit.

51

Sure the introducer covered the high points; however, he didn't provide her with a lead-in that would have gotten the audience excited to hear what she was going to be talking about. Remember: your introduction is really **your opening act**. Since you are the one who cares the most about it, you need to write it out and give it to the person who will be introducing you.

Pam had a great voice and she was easy to hear. The challenge was that she was somewhat **difficult to find**. She strolled across the stage from side to side while she was talking leaving the audience feeling like they were watching a tennis match.

Her information was great, but her PowerPoint slides were not. On one slide I counted 15 text bullets — way too many to cram onto a single slide and way too many to expect an audience to read. I'll be the first to admit that Pam had a challenge here — she was reviewing federal laws and they tend to be **both lengthy and detailed**. However, that doesn't mean that your slides need to be that way. Break it up and use multiple slides if you have to.

The one thing that Pam did better than any of the other speakers who spoke that day was to **use stories**. Once again, a lot of what she was talking about was issues related to federal policy and that can be a bit dry. However, she added stories that were both motivational (you've got to make changes) as well as relative ("my customers are telling me..."). This really helped to make her speech stand out.

Dr. Jay Wolfson

Dr. Jay Wolfson Speaks

Dr. Wolfson was, in a word, a character. He started off his presentation by telling the audience that he's been a university teacher for over 25 years and **it really showed in his presentation**. He seemed to feel at home standing behind the podium and he had clearly done this before.

Dr. Wolfson exuded energy. From the forcefulness of his voice to his rapid hand gestures you could see that he not only knew his subject well, but he also **cared deeply about it.**

For such a high-energy person, it must have been frustrating to have to be **tied to the podium**, which is where the microphone was. However he dealt with it gracefully and only occasionally had to restrain himself from going for a stroll.

For such a great presenter, you'd hope that the supporting slides would be of the same quality. Nope, once again the slides clearly had not been designed to do what PowerPoint slides should do — support the speaker. Instead, odd fonts had been used and too much small text had been crammed into each slide. I believe that these slides **may have looked fine on a computer monitor**; however, once they were displayed for a large audience they showed their flaws.

What All Of This Means For You

Hopefully you can take heart from this report back from the front lines of public speaking — even really well educated people could stand to improve their speaking skills. Both Ms. Arlotto and Dr. Wolfson really knew their material well, it's just that their presentations **could have used some help**.

The next time that you give a speech, make sure that you are prepared to **stand where they tell you to**. Whether it's anchored behind a podium or anywhere on a stage, you'll need to adapt your speaking style to match it.

Finally, although we all have mixed feelings about PowerPoint slides these two presentations clearly show that when you create a deck of slides **you need a second opinion**. Taking the time to run your slides by a colleague can do wonders for your ability to successfully connect with your audience.

Chapter 12

Charisma: What It Is, How To Get It, And Why You Want It

Chapter 12: Charisma: What It Is, How To Get It, And Why You Want It

So here's a quiz for you: who has been the best speaker in the past 100 years? Not an easy question to answer, eh? Even those of us who don't spend a lot of time studying history can come up with an impressive list of names: John F. Kennedy, Nelson Mandela, Martin Luther King, Adolf Hitler (even mean people can be good speakers), Winston Churchill, etc. Clearly these are the best of the best when it comes to speaking in public. **What made them so good** and can we become as good as they were?

What Is Charisma?

It turns out that in addition to being in the right place at the right time, these fantastic speakers all shared one thing in common: **they had charisma**. In a nutshell, a speaker who has charisma has the ability to connect with their audience and cause their emotions to be induced into the audience.

Eva Kihlstrom has studied what it takes to obtain charisma and she's discovered that 50% of our charisma is built into our genetic make-up — we've either got it or we don't, **the other 50% can be learned**. Let's see what we can do about the part that can be learned...

It's All About Technique

We've all seen speakers who didn't have charisma — they were no fun to either watch or listen to. The reason that we didn't like being in their audience is because they spoke with a monotone voice and displayed almost no emotion. **Clearly they weren't connecting with us.**

In order to work more of that powerful charisma stuff into your next speech, you need to start to **vary your voice** to match what you are talking about. If you are trying to convey fear, then you need to raise your voice. If you are trying to communicate wisdom, then take it down a few notches.

Your face needs to match the words that are coming out of your mouth. So much of our emotions are played out over our faces that if you can use your face to its fullest extent while you are delivering your speech, then you'll be able to draw your audience into the emotions that go along with your story.

Have Your Body Tell The Right Story

Hopefully you are getting the point that charisma is so hard to do because it's really the result of **using everything that you've got** to deliver your speech. This includes using your entire body: how you move on stage, the tone of your voice as you speak, in addition to the actual words that you use in speech that you deliver.

The difference between a speaker with charisma and one who doesn't have it can be striking. A speaker who has charisma speaks with **so much energy** that the audience can't help but get caught up in the topic. It's this energy that can motivate an audience to go out and take action based on what was said.

Mental Images Rule

In order to connect with an audience, a charismatic speaker needs to be able to **build vivid images** in their audience's minds. Having a shared mental image can do remarkable things in terms of bringing an audience closer to a speaker.

In order to create a clear image, a speaker needs to pick their words carefully. Using words that have **easily pictured images** makes this much easier to do. Take some time and listen to (or read) great speeches from charismatic speakers and you'll see that this is exactly what they do.

What All Of This Means For You

Once you get over the nerves and jitters that come with speaking in public, we all start to wonder **what comes next**. The ultimate goal for any speaker is to start to work more charisma into your speaking style.

In order to do this, you need to find ways to make **a stronger connection with your audiences**. No new technology is needed to make this happen. What you need to do is to make better use of your voice, your facial expressions, and your body language.

The power of a charismatic speaker is impressive. If you take the time to work on developing your skills in this area, then you will have a skill that very few speakers can demonstrate and this will make you stand out from everyone else.

It's from the forge of failure that the steel of success is formed.

Hard Work Does Not Guarantee Success, But Success Does Not Happen Without Hard Work.

- Dr. Jim Anderson

Create Speeches That Motivate Your Audiences And Get Your Message Heard!

Dr. Jim Anderson is available to provide training and coaching on the topics that are the most important to people who have to speak in public: how can I create a speech that people want to hear and how can I deliver in a way that will allow me to connect with my audience and get my point across to them?

Dr. Anderson believes that in order to both learn and remember what he says, speakers need to laugh. Each one of his speeches is full of fun and humor so that what he says "sticks" with everyone.

Dr. Anderson's Public Speaking Training Includes:

1. How to plan your next speech: pick your purpose and understand your audience.
2. What's the best way to get PowerPoint and Keynote to work with you, not against you?
3. What do you need to do when you are presenting in order to truly connect with your audience?

Dr. Jim Anderson presents over 100 speeches per year. To invite Dr. Anderson to speak at your event, contact him at: **Phone: 813-418-6970** or **Email: jim@BlueElephantConsulting.com**

Blue Elephant Consulting

Speaking.   Negotiating.   Managing.   Marketing.

Photo Credits:

Cover - By: Dawn Perry
http://www.flickr.com/photos/dawn_perry/

Chapter 1 - By: Internet Archive Book Images
https://www.flickr.com/photos/internetarchivebookimages/

Chapter 2 - By: redsoul300
http://www.flickr.com/photos/23963573@N08/

Chapter 3 - By: Andres Ubierna
http://www.flickr.com/photos/andresubierna/

Chapter 4 - By: ason Meredith
http://www.flickr.com/photos/merfam/

Chapter 5 - By: TechShowNetwork
http://www.flickr.com/photos/techshownetwork/

Chapter 6 - By: Peter Prehn
http://www.flickr.com/photos/pictoscribe/

Chapter 7 - By: Giulia Forsythe
http://www.flickr.com/photos/gforsythe/

Chapter 8 - By: Political Graveyard
http://www.flickr.com/photos/politicalgraveyard/

Chapter 9 - By: kioan
http://www.flickr.com/photos/kioan/

Chapter 10 - By: Eric Stensland Smith
http://www.flickr.com/photos/stenz/

Chapter 11 - By: Damon Sacks
http://www.flickr.com/photos/damonsacks/

Chapter 12 - By: Wikipedia
http://en.wikipedia.org/wiki/File:Martin_Luther_King_Jr_NYWT S.jpg

Other Books By The Author

Product Management

- Product Management Secrets: Techniques For Product Managers To Boost Product Sales And Increase Customer Satisfaction

- Product Development Lessons For Product Managers: How Product Managers Can Create Successful Products

- Customer Lessons For Product Managers: Techniques For Product Managers To Better Understand What Their Customers Really Want

- Product Failure Lessons For Product Managers: Examples Of Products That Have Failed For Product Managers To Learn From

- Communication Skills For Product Managers: The Communication Skills That Product Managers Need To Know How To Use In Order To Have A Successful Product

- How To Have A Successful Product Manager Career: The Things That You Need To Be Doing TODAY In Order To Have A Successful Product Manager Career

- Product Manager Product Success: How to keep your product on track and make it become a success

- Sales Secrets For Product Managers: Tips & Techniques For Product Managers To Better Understand How To Sell Their Product

Public Speaking

- How To Give A Great Presentation: Presentation techniques that will transform a speech into a memorable event

- How To Rehearse In Order To Give The Perfect Speech: How to effectively rehearse your next speech to that your message be remembered forever!

- Secrets To Creating The Perfect Speech: How to create a speech that will make your message be remembered forever!

- Secrets To Organizing The Perfect Speech: How to organize the best speech of your life!

- Secrets To Planning The Perfect Speech: How to plan to give the best speech of your life

- How To Show What You Mean During A Presentation: How to use visual techniques to transform a speech into a memorable event

CIO Skills

- What CIOs Need To Know About Working With Partners: Techniques For CIOs To Use In Order To Be Able To Successfully Work With Partners

- Critical CIO Management Skills: Decision Making Skills That Every CIO Needs To Have In Order To Be Able To Make The Right Choices

- How CIOs Can Make Innovation Happen: Tips And Techniques For CIOs To Use In Order To Make Innovation Happen In Their IT Department

- CIO Communication Skills Secrets: Tips And Techniques For CIOs To Use In Order To Become Better Communicators

- Managing Your CIO Career: Steps That CIOs Have To Take In Order To Have A Long And Successful Career

- CIO Business Skills: How CIOs can work effectively with the rest of the company!

IT Manager Skills

- How IT Managers Can Make Innovation Happen: Tips And Techniques For IT Managers To Use In Order To Make Innovation Happen In Their Teams

- Staffing Skills IT Managers Must Have: Tips And Techniques That IT Managers Can Use In Order To Correctly Staff Their Teams

- Secrets Of Effective Leadership For IT Managers: Tips And Techniques That IT Managers Can Use In Order To Develop Leadership Skills

- IT Manager Career Secrets: Tips And Techniques That IT Managers Can Use In Order To Have A Successful Career

- IT Manager Budgeting Skills: How IT Managers Can Request, Manage, Use, And Track Their Funding

Negotiating

- Learn How To Signal In Your Next Negotiation: How To Develop The Skill Of Effective Signaling In A Negotiation In Order To Get The Best Possible Outcome

- Learn The Skill Of Exploring In A Negotiation: How To Develop The Skill Of Exploring What Is Possible In A Negotiation In Order To Reach The Best Possible Deal

- Learn How To Argue In Your Next Negotiation: How To Develop The Skill Of Effective Arguing In A Negotiation In Order To Get The Best Possible Outcome

- How To Open Your Next Negotiation: How To Start A Negotiation In Order To Get The Best Possible Outcome

- Preparing For Your Next Negotiation: What You Need To Do BEFORE A Negotiation Starts In Order To Get The Best Possible Deal

Miscellaneous

- The Internet-Enabled Successful School District Superintendent: How To Use The Internet To Boost Parental Involvement In Your Schools

- Power Distribution Unit (PDU) Secrets: What Everyone Who Works In A Data Center Needs To Know!

- Making The Jump: How To Land Your Dream Job When You Get Out Of College!

"Change techniques that will transform a speech into a memorable event

This book has been written with one goal in mind – to show you how you can present a powerful and effective speech We're going to show you how to use the tools that every speaker has to deliver a great speech!

Let's Make Your Next Speech A Success!

What You'll Find Inside:

- **IT'S AMAZING WHAT A SPEAKER CAN LEARN BY WATCHING YOUTUBE**

- **YOU HAVE MUCH TO LEARN GRASSHOPPER: WHAT THE GREAT COMMUNICATORS CAN TEACH US**

- **PRESENTATION PRUNING: HOW MUCH TO CHOP?**

- **A PRESENTER'S GREATEST THREAT: SELF-SABOTAGE!**

Dr. Jim Anderson brings his 25 years of real-world experience to this book. He's delivered speeches at some of the world's largest firms as well as at many conferences. He's going to show you what you need to do in order to make your next speech a success!